You Can Order Pizza If It Sucks

a recipe book by rachel doherty

Copyright

First Edition

ISBN 9798343777789

To my momma and my late dad -

Mom, you instilled the drive and importance of home-cooked meals every night. I would watch you come home after a long day at work and immediately start prepping in the kitchen. Thank you for serving your family the way you do.

Dad, I'm not sure if it was taught or inherited but the art of throwing things together without measuring has been passed down, and I am forever grateful. I hope this makes you proud.

Contents

Introduction

Okay, let's start with the title "You Can Order Pizza If It Sucks" - these are the words my husband spoke to me in 2015 after a move across the country, pregnant with our first, and living on our own for the first time. From the beginning, he encouraged me to be as adventurous as I wanted in the kitchen, because, you know what... if it turned out terrible, we could always order pizza! At one point, we were choosing a world country and cooking from their most popular dishes that week. In all the trial and error, the real joy was found in the attempt and the act of serving my family.

The most intimidating part of creating this recipe book was realizing I had to start measuring and recording all my ingredients. I am notorious for never accurately measuring anything (hence this is mostly about cooking and not baking!) But now that I've done all the measuring for you, feel free to make them your own. Add extra cayenne, swap in your favorite cheese, use whatever cut of meat you have on hand, Google substitutions; cooking is an adventure, have fun with it!

During this stage of life (young kids, busy schedules), I find some shortcuts are worth the convenience. The first being pre-made pie crusts - graham cracker and pastry. Second, salad dressings - we love a good salad (see page 34) but the majority of our salad dressing is store bought. Our favorites include Kroger Private Selection raspberry vinaigrette, Aldi house Italian, and Cardini's caesar. Kroger Private selection marinara is our go-to for any red sauce, whether it be pasta or pizza. Lastly, in replace of bottled sriracha sauce, I've found that McCormick sriracha seasoning not only takes up less space but is the perfect way to add a bit of heat to truly ANY meal.

Absolute must-haves for your kitchen and for some of these recipes: a dutch oven, parchment paper (goodbye foil!), cast iron skillet, dry & liquid measuring cups, a blender or food processor, air fryer, mesh strainer, and a hand or stand mixer.

Appetizers & Sides

Broccoli Salad

INGREDIENTS

- 1/2 lb bacon
- 3 broccoli crowns
- 1/2 cup red onion
- 1 cup mayonnaise
- 1 Tbsp sugar
- 2 Tbsp honey
- 1/2 cup craisins
- 1/2 cup sunflower seeds
- 3/4 cup shredded cheddar cheese

DIRECTIONS

1. Cook bacon until crisp. Crumble and set aside.
2. Cut broccoli into bite-sized pieces, and finely dice the red onion.
3. In a large bowl, combine mayonnaise, sugar, and honey. Add chopped broccoli and onion, stir until evenly distributed.
4. Add craisins, sunflower seeds, shredded cheese, and crumbled bacon. Stir and chill until ready to serve.

Famous Brussels

INGREDIENTS

- 1-1 ½ lb brussels sprouts
- 1/2 lb bacon
- 2 Tbsp butter
- Honey
- Balsamic glaze

DIRECTIONS

1. Preheat oven to 400 degrees.
2. Trim and halve each brussel, removing any outer leaves.
3. Cut bacon into 1-inch pieces, brown in an oven proof skillet until starting to crisp. Do not drain any bacon fat, it will add extra flavor!
4. Add brussels and cook until browned on all sides, adding butter as needed.
5. Put pan in preheated oven until soft, about 15-20 minutes.
6. To finish, drizzle with honey and balsamic glaze.

Baked Goat Cheese Dip

INGREDIENTS

- 8 oz goat cheese log
- 8 oz cream cheese
- 1 Tbsp honey
- 1/2 tsp garlic powder
- 1 tsp herbs de provence
- 1/2 tsp salt
- 1/2 tsp red pepper flakes
- 1/4 cup parmesan

DIRECTIONS

1. Let goat cheese and cream cheese come to room temperature, about 30 minutes.
2. Preheat oven to 400 degrees.
3. With a hand mixer, whip the goat cheese, cream cheese, and honey together.
4. Add the rest of the ingredients and mix with a spatula.
5. Transfer to a small baking dish and bake for 15-20 minutes.
6. Serve warm with tortilla chips or sliced baguettes. If desired, drizzle with extra honey or hot honey for an added kick!

Note—you can easily double this recipe for a crowd! Try it with any fresh herbs, cranberries, marinara, and/or red peppers!

Air-Fried Buffalo Cauliflower

INGREDIENTS

- 1 head of cauliflower (about 4 cups)

for the sauce
- 1/2 cup butter
- 1/2 cup Redhot hot sauce
- 1/4 tsp garlic powder
- 1/4 tsp salt
- 1 tsp Worcestershire sauce
- 1/2 tsp apple cider vinegar
- 1 tsp sugar

for the batter
- 1/2 cup flour
- 1/2 cup cornstarch
- 1/2 tsp baking powder
- 1/2 tsp salt
- 1/4 tsp pepper
- 1/4 tsp garlic powder
- 1/4 tsp onion powder
- 1 cup seltzer water

- Ranch, for serving

to make your own
-Mix ranch seasoning packet with 1/2 buttermilk and 1/2 cup mayo. Add salt and pepper to taste.

DIRECTIONS

1. Chop the cauliflower into bite-size pieces.
2. Heat sauce ingredients in a small pan and keep warm.
3. Whisk batter ingredients together, adding the seltzer last, until just combined.
4. Preheat air fryer at 400 degrees for 5 minutes.
5. Toss the cauliflower into the batter. Working in two batches, cook in air fryer for 10-15 minutes, tossing halfway through.
6. While still hot, toss the cauliflower in the sauce and serve immediately.

Northern Cornbread

INGREDIENTS

- 1 box Jiffy cornbread
- 1/4 cup sugar
- 1/2 stick butter, softened
- 1 egg
- 1/3 cup milk
- 1 Tbsp canola oil

DIRECTIONS

1. Place a medium sized cast iron in the oven to preheat at 400 degrees.
2. In a small bowl, mix softened butter and sugar until smooth. Add in jiffy and stir.
3. Whisk egg and milk together and add to mixture until just blended.
4. Carefully remove cast iron from the oven. Add oil and then batter to the middle of the pan.
5. Bake for 20 minutes or until browned on top.

Note—while living in the north, we called this our "southern cornbread," but after moving and speaking with southerners, it turns out they like their sweet tea sweet but their cornbread savory. So enjoy our sweet northern cornbread recipe.

Bacon-tizers

INGREDIENTS

- 1/2 pound of thick-cut bacon
- 1/3 cup of brown sugar
- Jarred jalapeños
- Club crackers

DIRECTIONS

1. Preheat oven to 350 degrees.
2. Lay out crackers on a parchment lined baking sheet.
3. Cut bacon to the size of the cracker.
4. In a small bowl, toss bacon with brown sugar.
5. To assemble, place sugared bacon and jalapeños on top of each cracker.
6. Bake for 25-30 minutes. Enjoy warm!

Mediterranean Orzo Salad

INGREDIENTS

- 1 lb orzo
- 1 bottle garlic expressions
- 1 can chickpeas
- 2-3 bell peppers
- 1/2 red onion
- 2-3 ears corn, raw
- Cherry tomatoes
- 4-6 oz feta cheese
- juice of 1/2 lemon
- 1/4 cup fresh parsley
- 1/4 tsp each: salt, pepper, oregano

DIRECTIONS

1. Cook orzo to al dente and rinse with cold water. Place in a large bowl and add in the bottle of garlic expressions, removing any whole garlic cloves. Stir.
2. Dice the bell pepper and onion, cut corn off the cob, halve tomatoes, rinse chickpeas, and combine with the orzo.
3. Add feta, lemon juice, and herbs. Stir to combine and chill until ready to serve.

Note—adding raw corn to any cold salad gives such a great crunch!

Sweet & Spicy Chex Mix

INGREDIENTS

- 1 bag goldfish
- 1 bag popcorn
- 5 cups rice chex
- 5 cups corn chex
- 3 cups pretzels
- 4 Tbsp butter
- 4 Tbsp refined coconut oil
- 1 tsp cayenne
- 1 ½ tsp paprika
- 1 tsp garlic powder
- 2 Tbsp brown sugar

DIRECTIONS

1. Preheat oven to 250 degrees.
2. Combine first 5 ingredients in a roasting pan or foil pan.
3. Melt butter and coconut oil together. Combine all seasonings and mix with the melted butter, and stir. Pour over chex mix and stir until evenly coated.
4. Bake for 45 minutes, stirring every 15 minutes.
5. Spread out onto parchment paper or foil. Let cool (if you can wait) and enjoy!

Note—the secrets out... this may be my most requested recipe!

Foolproof Bread

INGREDIENTS

- 3 cups flour, plus 1 Tbsp
- 2 tsp salt
- 1 ½ tsp active dry yeast
- 1 ½ cups warm water

Note—if you mess this one up, pizza's on me!

DIRECTIONS

1. Combine 3 cups flour, salt, and yeast to a bowl. Stir with wooden spoon. Pour in warm water and mix until a ball forms. The dough should be sticky.
2. Cover bowl and let sit overnight or at least 8 hours.
3. With floured hands, punch down dough. Quickly form back into a ball and transfer to a piece of parchment paper. Sprinkle with flour, cover with plastic wrap, and let rest for 30 more minutes.
4. Meanwhile, place a dutch oven with the lid on in the oven and let preheat to 450 degrees.
5. Carefully remove lid, transfer the bread with the parchment paper to the preheated dutch oven. Replace lid and bake for 40 minutes.
6. Transfer bread to a cutting board and let cool for 15 minutes before slicing.

Bread Dipping Oil

INGREDIENTS

- High quality olive oil
- 1/2 tsp garlic powder
- 1/2 tsp salt
- 1/4 tsp pepper
- 1/2 tsp red pepper flakes
- 1/2 tsp onion powder
- 1 Tbsp oregano
- 1 Tbsp basil
- 1 Tbsp parsley

DIRECTIONS

1. Mix all seasonings together and stir to combine.
2. Use 1 tsp of seasonings per 4 Tbsp oil.
3. Store leftover seasoning mix in the refrigerator.

Parm Crusted Potatoes

INGREDIENTS

- 24 oz bag of petite gold potatoes
- 2 Tbsp butter
- 1 ½ cups fresh parmesean cheese
- 1 ½ tsp Italian seasoning
- 1/2 tsp red pepper flakes, optional
- Salt + pepper

DIRECTIONS

1. Boil potatoes in salted water until fork tender, about 15 minutes. Drain and let cool to touch.
2. Grate parmesan cheese and half each potato. Heat butter in a non-stick skillet to medium-high heat.
3. Cover the bottom of the pan the cheese, sprinkle Italian seasoning and red pepper flakes if using.. Place potatoes cut side down, spray with olive oil and season the tops of the potatoes with salt and pepper. Let cook until cheese is crispy, about 5 minutes.

Blended Salsa

INGREDIENTS

- 4 ripe heirloom tomatoes
- 1-3 jalapeños, depending on spice preference
- 1 small red onion
- 2 garlic cloves
- 1/2 cup fresh cilantro
- Juice of 1 lime
- 4 tsp sugar
- 2 ½ tsp salt
- 15 oz can of crushed tomatoes
- 4 oz can of green chilies, hot or mild

DIRECTIONS

1. Quarter tomatoes and red onion. Cut jalapeños, remove and set aside seeds.
2. Add all ingredients to a blender or food processor, blend until mostly smooth. Work in batches if necessary.
3. Stir in all or some of the jalapeño seeds according to the spice level you desire.
4. Chill until ready to serve.

Rustic Warm Potato Salad

INGREDIENTS

- 2 lbs petite potatoes
- 1 Tbsp butter
- 1 Tbsp olive oil
- 1/2 lb bacon
- 1 shallot, chopped
- 1/3 cup mayonnasise
- 1/4 cup plain yogurt or sour cream
- 1/4 tsp salt
- 1/8 tsp pepper
- 1/8 tsp cayenne
- 1/2 Tbsp pickle juice
- 1 tsp dijon
- Green onions

DIRECTIONS

1. Preheat oven to 425 degrees. Quarter the potatoes and toss in olive oil and butter on a baking sheet. Roast for 25 minutes, tossing halfway through.
2. Cook bacon until crisp, crumble, and set aside.
3. Leaving 2 tsp bacon grease in the pan, sauté shallot until soft.
4. In a large bowl, combine mayonnaise, yogurt/sour cream, salt, pepper, cayenne, pickle juice, and dijon mustard.
5. Add roasted potatoes, shallots, and bacon to the bowl, toss. Top with green onions and serve warm.

Buffalo Chicken Dip

INGREDIENTS

- 4 10 oz cans of chicken
- 8 oz cream cheese
- 3/4 cup ranch dressing
- 5 oz franks red hot sauce
- 1 cup shredded cheddar

DIRECTIONS

1. Drain cans of chicken.
2. Combine all ingredients into small crock pot.
3. Heat on low until cream cheese is fully melted, about 1 hour. Stir until fully combined.
4. Serve with tortilla chips, crackers, or celery sticks.

Note—add a scoop to level up your grilled cheese!

Lemon Feta
Roasted Broccoli Salad

INGREDIENTS

- 3 heads of broccoli
- Olive oil
- Salt + pepper
- 4-6 oz pancetta
- 1 Tbsp butter
- 2-3 slices bread, cut into cubes
- 1/2 cup crumbled feta cheese
- zest from 1/2 a lemon
- 1 tsp garlic

DIRECTIONS

1. Preheat oven to 400 degrees.
2. Wash and chop broccoli into 1-inch pieces, toss in olive oil, salt, and pepper.
3. Place broccoli on one side of a baking sheet and the pancetta on the other. Roast until pancetta is crisp and broccoli is tender, about 25-30 minutes.
4. Remove from oven and transfer to a bowl. Add butter to the hot baking sheet and toss bread to coat. Toast for 10 minutes.
5. While everything is still warm, add in feta, lemon zest, and garlic. Serve immediately.

Southern Sausage Balls

INGREDIENTS

- 1 lb ground sausage
- 2 cups bisquick
- 4 oz cream cheese, softened
- 12 oz pimento cheese

DIRECTIONS

1. Preheat the oven to 350 degrees.
2. Combine all ingredients in a large bowl. Use your hands to mix, and form into 1 inch balls.
3. Place on a parchment lined baking sheet, bake for 20-25 minutes.

Makes 24 sausage balls

Poppyseed Dressing

INGREDIENTS

- 1/4 cup red onion, quartered
- 1/2 tsp salt
- 1/4 tsp mustard powder
- 1 ½ Tbsp sugar
- 1 Tbsp honey
- 2 Tbsp apple cider vinegar
- 1/4 cup white vinegar
- 1 Tbsp poppy seeds
- 1/2-1 cup vegetable oil

DIRECTIONS

1. In blender or food processor, blend first 7 ingredients. Add in oil (starting with ½ cup and adding more to your liking) and poppy seeds, and pulse to combine.
2. Transfer to container and chill until ready to use. Be sure to shake before use, separation is normal.

Our fav spinach salads:

Apple Feta:
chopped spinach, chopped honey crisp apples, pomegranate seeds, crumbled feta, sliced almonds, Aldi house Italian

Strawberry Goat Cheese:
chopped spinach, sliced strawberries, crumbled goat cheese, pecans, Kroger Private Selection raspberry vinaigrette

Orange Poppyseed:
chopped spinach, canned mandarin oranges, sliced almonds, thinly sliced red onion, poppyseed dressing (above)

Caesar:
chopped spinach, croutons, fresh parmesan cheese, Cardini's caesar dressing

Sparkling Grapes

INGREDIENTS

- Seedless red grapes
- 1 cup Welch's sparkling grape juice
- 3 Tbsp sugar

DIRECTIONS

1. Destem and wash grapes.
2. Place grapes in a bowl and cover with grape juice.
3. Marinate in the fridge 8-24 hours.
4. Drain and toss grapes in sugar.
5. Place in the freezer for at least 2 hours.
6. Serve frozen.

Note—try with green grapes and sparkling white grape juice!

Mains

Boursin Pasta

INGREDIENTS

- 1 head of broccoli
- 1 bunch of asparagus
- Olive oil
- Salt + pepper
- 1/4 tsp onion powder
- 1/4 tsp ground mustard
- 1 head of garlic
- 1 small lemon
- Boursin Shallot & Chive Cheese
- 1/4 cup pine nuts
- 1/2 lb rigatoni, or other short cut pasta
- Fresh basil and parmesan cheese

DIRECTIONS

1. Preheat oven to 400 degrees.
2. Chop broccoli and asparagus into 1 inch pieces, arrange on baking sheet and toss with olive oil, salt, pepper, onion powder, and ground mustard.
3. Slice off the top of the garlic to expose the cloves and cut the lemon in half. Place on the pan and drizzle with olive oil. Place Boursin cheese in the center of vegetables. Bake for 30 minutes, adding the pine nuts in the last 5 minutes to toast.
4. Meanwhile, cook pasta according to package instructions. Reserve 1/2 cup pasta water.
5. Keeping everything on the baking sheet, squeeze lemon juice and garlic cloves out directly onto the cheese, mash with a fork. Add the pasta water and mix to create a creamy sauce, add pasta and toss together.
6. Top with parmesan and basil to serve.

Grown-Up Grilled Cheese

INGREDIENTS

- Brioche buns
- Butter

combinations pictured

- pear, smoked gouda, honey
- bacon, brie, apple
- raspberry jam, brie, white cheddar

other ingredients to consider

- caramelized onion
- dijon mustard
- roasted garlic
- sun-dried tomatoes
- mushrooms
- swiss cheese
- mozzarella
- pepper jack cheese

DIRECTIONS

1. Heat a skillet to medium heat.
2. Butter the *inside* of each bun. Place butter side down, layer your favorite ingredients, and top with top bun, butter side up.
3. Let cook until each side is browned and cheese is melted. Enjoy!

Pizza Salad

INGREDIENTS

for the dressing
- 2 Tbsp olive oil
- Salt + pepper
- 1/4 cup red wine vinegar
- 1/2 tsp dijon mustard
- 1 Tbsp honey
- 1 Tbsp pepperoncini juice
- 1/4 tsp garlic powder
- 1/4-1/2 tsp dried basil
- 1/4 tsp oregano

for the salad
- 1/4 lb deli pepperoni
- 3 oz mozzarella slices
- 1/4 cup shredded parmesan
- 1 Tbsp shallot or red onion
- 3 pepperoncinis, sliced
- 1/2 pint cherry tomatoes
- 1/2-1 lb brussels sprouts

DIRECTIONS

1. Whisk dressing ingredients together and set aside.
2. Trim and thinly slice brussels sprouts.
3. Cut pepperoni and mozzarella cheese into thin strips. Halve tomatoes.
4. Combine all ingredients in a large bowl and toss with the dressing.
5. If desired, top with extra parmesan cheese and red pepper flakes. Serve cold.

INGREDIENTS

- 1/2 lb bacon
- 2 large carrots
- 1 shallot
- 1 ½ lbs ground beef
- 1 lb ground sausage
- 1 tsp salt
- 1/2 tsp pepper
- 2/3 cup red wine
- 1 jar marinara
- 2 Tbsp tomato paste
- 1/2 tsp Italian seasoning
- 1/4 tsp ground cloves
- 1/4 tsp cinnamon
- 4 oz baby bella mushrooms, sliced
- 6 oz cream cheese, cubed
- 8-10 oven ready lasagna noodles
- 8 oz fresh mozzarella, sliced

Not Your Mother's Lasagna

DIRECTIONS

1. Cut bacon into bite size pieces. Crisp over M-H heat in a dutch oven or other large ovenproof skillet. Dice carrots and shallot, add to bacon and cook for 5 minutes.
2. Add ground beef, sausage, salt and pepper. Stir to break up meat, cooking until no longer pink. Drain off ½ cup grease if needed.
3. Add wine and cook for 5 minutes. Add marinara and tomato paste, Italian seasoning, cloves, and cinnamon. Simmer for 5 more minutes.
4. Stir in mushrooms and cream cheese until melted.
5. Preheat oven to 350 degrees.
6. Break noodles into 3-4 pieces and start arranging them in the sauce, pushing them to the bottom to create a flat layer. Alternate noodles and fresh mozzarella slices until all are used. Place any extra mozzarella on the top.
7. Bake for 25-30 minutes, and let cool for 10 minutes. Top with basil and enjoy!

Note—the cloves and cinnamon are optional, but they make any red sauce dish so much cozier- especially during the holidays! Try it out!

Bacon-Wrapped Meatloaves

INGREDIENTS

- 2 lbs ground beef
- 2 Tbsp worcestershire
- 1 egg
- 1 Tbsp minced onion, or 1 tsp onion powder
- 2 tsp garlic powder
- 1 cup panko breadcrumbs
- 6 thin bacon slices
- 1/2 cup ketchup
- 1 Tbsp dijon mustard
- 2 Tbsp brown sugar

DIRECTIONS

1. Combine first 6 ingredients into a bowl. Mix thoroughly with hands and form into six equal parts. Form into a ball and flatten slightly. Place on a parchment lined baking sheet.
2. Wrap each meatloaf with a piece of bacon.
3. Mix ketchup, dijon, and brown sugar into a small bowl. Spoon over meatloaves.
4. Bake at 375 for 45 minutes.

Makes personal 6 meatloaves

Salmon Rub

INGREDIENTS

for 1 lb of salmon
- 1 Tbsp brown sugar
- 1/4 tsp pepper
- 1/2 tsp coarse salt
- 1/4 tsp basil
- 1/4 tsp garlic powder
- 1/4 tsp smoked paprika
- Lime zest

DIRECTIONS

1. Mix all ingredients together in a small bowl.
2. Pat salmon dry and generously season with rub.
3. Bake salmon at 375 degrees for 13-15 minutes or until internal temperature reaches 145 degrees.

Sushi Bake

INGREDIENTS

- 1 1/2 cup basmati rice
- 1-2 tsp sesame oil
- 1/3 cup rice vinegar
- 1/2 Tbsp sugar
- 1 tsp salt
- 1 Tbsp sesame seeds
- Sriracha seasoning or red pepper flakes
- 2 oz cream cheese, room temperature
- 1/2 cup mayonnaise
- 1 egg yolk
- 1 tsp dijon mustard
- 1/2 tsp salt
- 1 tsp sugar
- 1 Tbsp rice vinegar
- 2 tsp lemon juice
- 12 oz salad shrimp
- 16 oz imitation crab meat
- 1/2 cup panko bread crumbs

DIRECTIONS

1. Rinse rice until water runs clear, and cook according to package directions.
2. Preheat oven to 425 degrees. Lightly spray a 9x12 dish with cooking oil and drizzle sesame oil over the bottom of the dish.
3. Heat rice vinegar, sugar, and salt on low heat until sugar is dissolved.
4. Mix prepared rice with the warm vinegar mixture and place in prepared dish. Sprinkle sesame seeds and desired amount of sriracha seasoning or red pepper flakes over the rice.
5. Combine cream cheese, mayo, egg yolk, dijon, salt, sugar, rice vinegar, and lemon juice in a medium bowl. Add shrimp and crab, and toss to coat. Spread evenly over the rice mixture.
6. Sprinkle the top with panko and more sriracha seasoning or red pepper flakes.
7. Bake 10-15 minutes or until warm.

INGREDIENTS

- 2 frozen deep dish pie crusts

for the base (makes 2)
- 5 whole eggs
- Pinch of red pepper flakes
- Salt + pepper
- 1/2 cup creme fraiche, or plain greek yogurt
- 1 tsp basil
- 1 tsp fresh chives
- 1 1/4 cup whole milk

for mushroom + asparagus + brie
- 4 oz sliced baby bella mushrooms
- 1/2 bunch asparagus
- 4 oz brie

for jalapeño + cheddar + charred corn
- 2 Tbsp jarred jalapeños
- 1/2 cup shredded cheddar
- 1/2 cup frozen charred corn

for caramelized onion + goat cheese + honey
- 1/2 sweet onion
- 1/2 log goat cheese
- 1 Tbsp honey

for mushroom + feta + sundried tomato + spinach
- 4 oz sliced baby bella mushrooms
- 3 Tbsp feta
- 1/4 cup sundried tomatoes
- Small handful of spinach

Quiche 4 Ways

DIRECTIONS

TO START- Thaw crusts at room temperature for 25 minutes. Prick with a fork to prevent bubbling and parbake for 10 minutes at 400 degrees. Whisk base ingredients and set aside.

for mushroom + asparagus + brie
- Cook mushrooms in 1/2 Tbsp butter until browned and juices are absorbed.
- Cut bottom 2 inches off the asparagus and discard, chop the rest into 1 inch pieces
- Cut rind off of brie and cut into cubes.
- Combine all ingredients into prepared crust. Drizzle with honey.

for jalapeño + cheddar + charred corn
- Combine all ingredients into prepared crust.

for caramelized onion + goat cheese + honey
- Thinly slice onion with sauté in 1 1/2 Tbsp butter until caramelized, about 10-15 minutes.
- Combine all ingredients into prepared crust.

for mushroom + feta + sundried tomato + spinach
- Cook mushrooms in 1/2 Tbsp butter until browned and juices are absorbed.
- Chop spinach and sun dried tomatoes into small pieces.

TO FINISH- Place both crusts on a large baking sheet. Divide the base mixture evenly into crusts and bake for 45-50 minutes.

INGREDIENTS

for the marinade
- 2 lbs chicken thighs
- 1 tsp garlic
- 1 tsp chili powder
- 1/2 tsp ground ginger
- 1 tsp salt

for the sauce
- 1 red onion, roughly chopped
- 2 Tbsp butter
- 3 Tbsp tomato paste
- 3 Tbsp cashews
- 1/2 cup water
- 2 Tbsp sugar
- Dash of cayenne
- 1/2 tsp chili powder
- 2 Tbsp apple cider vinegar
- 1 tsp garam masala
- 3 Tbsp cream, or whole milk
- 1 stick butter

for serving
- Basmati rice
- 15 oz ricotta
- 1 Tbsp lemon juice

Whipped Ricotta Butter Chicken

DIRECTIONS

1. Trim and cut chicken thighs into bite size pieces. Combine garlic, chili powder, ginger, salt and chicken into a bowl. Mix with hands to fully coat chicken, and let sit for 15 minutes.
2. Heat a large skillet to medium heat. Add 1 Tbsp oil and brown chicken. Transfer to plate. Work in batches if necessary.
3. In the same pan, combine all sauce ingredients and bring to a boil. Simmer for 15 minutes.
4. Meanwhile, rinse and start the rice.
5. Transfer sauce into a bowl, and add cream or milk. Using an immersion blender, blend until smooth.
6. Strain through a mesh strainer into the same skillet. Be patient with this part. Use a wooden spoon to stir and push down the sauce into the strainer. Don't forget to scrape the bottom of the strainer for the good stuff! Once completely transferred to the skillet, add stick of butter. Cook on low until butter is melted, add in chicken and any juices.
7. Whip ricotta and lemon juice together on medium speed for about 2 minutes. Enjoy!

Ground Beef Wellies

INGREDIENTS

- 1 box Pepperidge Farm Puff Pastry Sheets
- 8 oz baby bella mushrooms
- 1 small onion
- 3 Tbsp butter
- 2 tsp minced garlic
- 2 tsp dried basil
- 1/2 cup red wine
- 1 1/2 lbs ground beef
- 1/4 cup breadcrumbs
- 1 tsp salt
- 1 Tbsp dried parsley
- 2 eggs
- 1 Tbsp milk or cream

DIRECTIONS

1. Thaw puff pastry according to package instructions. Preheat oven to 400 degrees.
2. Finely chop mushrooms and onion. Melt butter in medium pan and sauté mushrooms and onions until soft. Add garlic, basil, and wine. Cook until wine is fully reduced, and let cool.
3. Combine ground beef, breadcrumbs, salt, parsley and eggs. Mix thoroughly with hands and divide into 8 equal balls, about 1/2 cup each.
4. Using a rolling pin, roll out each pastry sheet and cut into 4 equal squares - creating 8 total.
5. Assemble by putting 1 Tbsp mushroom mixture in the center of each pastry square and top with ground beef. Flatten sightly and fold the edge of the puff pastry around the filling and place seam side down on a parchment lined baking sheet.
6. Cut small slits in the top of each one, brush top and sides with milk or cream.
7. Bake 30-40 minutes, let cool 10 minutes before serving.

Makes 8 personal beef wellingtons

Gyro Burgers

INGREDIENTS

for the burgers
- 1 lb ground lamb
- 1/2 tsp salt
- 1/2 tsp pepper
- 1/2 tsp herbes de provence
- 1/4 tsp pumpkin pie spice or cinnamon
- 1/4 cup crumbled feta

to assemble
- Tzatziki sauce
- Jarred roasted red peppers
- Red onion, thinly sliced
- Brioche buns

DIRECTIONS

1. Combine burger ingredients into a bowl and mix with hands. Divide into 4 equal parts and shape into patties.
2. Grill burgers on medium-high for 5 minutes, flip and grill 5 more minutes.
3. Heat the roasted red peppers in a pan until warm. Toast buns if desired.
4. Top each burger with tzatziki, roasted red peppers, and sliced onion.

Lemon Butter Chicken Skewers

INGREDIENTS

- 1–1 ½ lbs chicken, boneless skinless thighs or breast

for the marinade

- 2 Tbsp olive oil
- 1/2 tsp salt
- 1/2 tsp pepper
- 1/2 tsp paprika
- 1 tsp garlic powder
- Zest of 1 lemon

for the lemon butter

- 5 Tbsp softened butter
- 1/2 tsp salt
- 1/4 tsp pepper
- 1 tsp sugar
- 1/4 tsp parsley flakes
- 2 tsp lemon juice

DIRECTIONS

1. Soak wooden skewers in water for at least 20 minutes.
2. Trim chicken and cut into 1-inch pieces.
3. Combine marinade ingredients and marinate chicken for 30 minutes, up to 2 hours.
4. Break skewers in half, tightly thread chicken on each skewer.
5. Combine the lemon butter ingredients, set aside.

air fry

Place in air fryer in a single layer, you may have to work in batches. Air fry at 400 degrees for 10 minutes, flip, and cook for 7-10 more minutes. Brush thoroughly with butter while still hot.

pan fry

Pan fry on medium-high until crisp on all sides and internal temperature reaches 165 degrees. Brush thoroughly with butter while still hot.

One Pot Chicken Gnocchi Soup

INGREDIENTS

- 1/2 onion
- 2 large carrots, or 8 baby
- 3 Tbsp butter
- 2 tsp minced garlic
- 3 10oz cans chicken, or rotisserie
- 6 cups chicken stock
- 1 cup chopped spinach
- 16oz package of gnocchi
- 2/3 cup heavy cream
- 1 cup freshly shredded parmesean
- Salt + pepper

DIRECTIONS

1. Chop onion and carrots into small pieces.
2. Melt butter in a large pot and sauté onion and carrots until soft, 5-10 minutes. Add garlic and sauté for 1 minute.
3. Drain the liquid from the cans of chicken. Add chicken and chicken stock to the pot. Let simmer for 15 minutes for the flavors to meld, stirring occasionally.
4. Add the spinach and gnocchi and let cook for 4-5 minutes.
5. Stir in the heavy cream and parmesan cheese until combined. Season with salt and pepper and serve!

Note—pairs perfectly with foolproof bread found on page 27.

Hot Honey & Ranch Chicken Naan

INGREDIENTS

- 3 Tbsp honey
- 1/2 tsp red pepper flakes
- 1/2 tsp hot sauce
- 4 mini naan
- 1 lb ground chicken
- 1 tsp garlic powder
- 1 tsp onion powder
- 1 tsp smoked paprika
- 4-6 slices colby jack cheese
- 1/2 cup shredded mozzerella
- Ranch for serving

DIRECTIONS

1. Mix honey, red pepper flakes, and hot sauce together. Set aside.
2. Cook ground chicken in a skillet, with garlic powder, onion powder, and smoked paprika.
3. Set oven to broil.
4. Place naan on a baking sheet, brush each one with honey mixture. Top with sliced colby jack cheese.
5. Spoon the ground chicken equally over each naan, top with mozzarella and broil until cheese is melted and bubbly, this will only take a few minutes.
6. Drizzle with ranch and more red pepper flakes, if desired.

Note— try using the homemade ranch recipe on page 18

INGREDIENTS

- 1 lb steak
- 1 lb gnocchi
- 1 Tbsp olive oil
- 2 Tbsp butter
- 1 tsp minced garlic
- 1 tsp parsley
- 1/4 cup shredded parmesan cheese

for the marinade

- 1 Tbsp olive oil
- 2 Tbsp worcestershire
- 1 tsp salt
- 1/2 tsp pepper
- Pinch of red pepper flakes
- 1 tsp onion powder
- 1 tsp garlic powder
- 1 tsp dijon mustard
- 1 Tbsp apple cider vinegar
- 1 Tbsp brown sugar

Steak and Gnocchi

DIRECTIONS

1. Trim and cut steak into bite size pieces. Combine marinade ingredients and marinade for at least one hour.
2. Boil gnocchi for 2 minutes. Strain and set aside.
3. Meanwhile, heat olive oil in a large cast iron skillet to medium high. Sear steak on all sides and transfer to a plate, cover.
4. Using the same skillet, turn heat to low. Add butter until browned, add gnocchi and cook for 1 min.
5. Combine steak back in and top with parsley and parmesan cheese. Serve immediately.

INGREDIENTS

for the marinade

- 1 lb chicken breast or thighs
- 2-3 Tbsp olive oil
- 1/2 Tbsp parsley
- 1/4 tsp salt
- 1/4 tsp pepper
- 1/4 tsp chili powder
- 1/2 tsp minced garlic

for the pasta

- 16 oz spaghetti noodles
- 6 Tbsp butter
- 1 shallot, chopped
- 5-6 fresh garlic cloves, about 1 Tbsp minced
- 1/2-1 tsp coarse ground pepper
- 1/2 tsp cayenne
- 2 tsp chili powder
- 1/2 tsp salt
- 1 cup freshly grated pecorino romano
- Parsley for garnish

Note - Try with grilled steak or shrimp!

Spicy Garlic Chicken Spaghetti

DIRECTIONS

1. Marinade chicken for at least 30 minutes. Grill or pan fry until internal temperature reaches 165 degrees.
2. Cook pasta al dente. Reserve 1 cup pasta water.
3. Melt butter on medium heat, add in shallots, fresh garlic. and coarse ground pepper. Sauté until soft.
4. Reduce heat to low and stir in cayenne, chili powder, and salt.
5. Remove from heat and add 1/2 cup pasta water and 1 cup cheese.
6. Toss noodles to evenly coat. Top with grilled chicken.

Cast Iron Pizza

INGREDIENTS

- Prepared pizza dough
- 1 Tbsp olive oil
- 1/2 lb mild sausage
- 1 log goat cheese, softened
- 1 Tbsp honey
- Red pepper flakes
- 1/4 red onion, diced
- 1/2 cup baby bella mushrooms, sliced
- 1/3 cup shredded mozzarella cheese
- Balsamic glaze

DIRECTIONS

1. Place cast iron in oven and preheat to 400 degrees.
2. Roll out the dough. Using a fork, poke holes in prepared dough to prevent bubbles from forming.
3. When oven is preheated, carefully remove cast iron. Pour 1 Tbsp olive oil in the bottom of the skillet and then place the dough in. Bake for 5 minutes.
4. Meanwhile, cook sausage until no longer pink. Stir together goat cheese, honey and red pepper flakes. Microwave for 10 seconds if it is too thick to spread.
5. Remove cast iron from the oven. Spread goat cheese mixture over the crust. Top with mozzarella cheese, cooked sausage, onions, and mushrooms. Bake for 10-15 more minutes.
6. Drizzle with balsamic glaze.

3-Hour Bagels

INGREDIENTS

- 1 ½ cup warm water
- 3¾ tsp active dry yeast
- 4 cups bread flour
- 1 Tbsp packed brown sugar
- 2 tsp salt
- Non-stick spray
- 1 egg, whisked
- 8-10 cups water
- 1/4 cup honey

DIRECTIONS

1. Whisk yeast and water in your mixing bowl, let sit for 5-10 minutes.
2. Add flour, brown sugar, and salt. Mix on low for 2 minutes. Remove to a floured surface. Knead the dough for about 3 minutes, or until the dough slightly bounces back when pressed.
3. Rub or spray oil over the dough ball and let sit in the bowl for 1 ½-2 hours, or until doubled in size. Line two baking sheets with parchment.
4. Punch down dough. Divide in half. Divide in half again, and again, until you have 8 dough balls. Using your thumb, create a hole in the middle of each one that is about 1 inch. Cover with a towel while doing the next step.
5. Preheat oven to 425 degrees. Fill a large pot with water and honey, bring to a low boil.
6. Drop bagel into water 4 at a time. Let float for 1 minute, flip, let float for 1 more minute.
7. Remove and place back on baking sheet. Brush all over with whisked egg. Bake for 12 minutes. Rotate and switch pan positions, bake for 8 more minutes. Cool on the baking sheet for 20 minutes. Enjoy!

Mini Dutch Babies

INGREDIENTS

- 2 Tbsp melted butter
- 1/2 cup whole milk
- 3 eggs
- 1/2 cup flour
- 1 ½ Tbsp sugar
- 1 tsp vanilla
- Pinch of salt

DIRECTIONS

1. Preheat oven to 450 degrees.
2. Melt butter in a medium bowl. Whisk in milk, then the remaining ingredients.
3. Thoroughly spray muffin tin and divide batter evenly into 12 muffin cups, about 2 Tbsp each.
4. Bake 10-15 minutes until they are puffed up and edges start to brown.
5. Top with powdered sugar and fresh fruit.

Note—a Dutch baby is a German style eggy pancake. I was first introduced to these by another military wife in 2016 and we have enjoyed them ever since. This "mini" version is so fun for the kids!

INGREDIENTS

- 2 lbs skirt or flank steak
- 1 large sweet potato
- 2 zucchini
- 1 tsp minced garlic
- Olive oil
- Pomegranate seeds

for the pomegranate reduction

- 15 oz pomegranate juice
- 1 Tbsp honey
- 2 Tbsp lemon juice
- 1/4 cup brown sugar
- 1 Tbsp balsamic vinegar

Pomegranate Steak Rolls

DIRECTIONS

1. Combine all sauce ingredients in a small saucepan and bring to a boil. Simmer on low for about an hour. Sauce will reduce by half and stick to the back of a spoon when ready.
2. Meanwhile, cut veggies into matchsticks. Heat oil in a large cast iron, stir fry the veggies for 5 minutes or until soft, adding in the garlic in the last minute.
3. Cut steak into strips, about 2 inches by 5 inches. To assemble, lay veggies on a strip of steak and roll. Secure with a toothpick.
4. In the same pan used for the veggies, heat 1 Tbsp olive oil and sear the steak rolls 1 minute on all sides, 4-5 minutes total. Keep pan covered while searing.
5. Remove toothpicks from each roll, top with sauce and pomegranate seeds.

Makes 10-12 rolls

Note—save any extra pomegranate reduction and drizzle on salad, fish, or grilled chicken.

Sips & Sweets

INGREDIENTS

- 2 sticks of butter, softened
- 1/4 tsp cinnamon
- 1/4 tsp allspice
- 1 ½ tsp rosewater
- 1 cup powdered sugar
- 2 cups flour
- Dark chocolate chips
- 2 Tbsp pistachios, chopped

Rosewater Shortbread Cookies

DIRECTIONS

1. In a stand mixer, whip the butter until fluffy, about 3 minutes.
2. Add in cinnamon, allspice, and rosewater on low. Slowly add powdered sugar. Beat for 2 more minutes. Add flour until combined.
3. Transfer dough onto large piece of plastic wrap and form into a log. Refrigerate for 2 hours.
4. Preheat oven to 325 degrees. Unwrap dough and slice into ¼ in slices.
5. Bake for 16-20 minutes, the outsides should be slightly browned. Let cool.
6. Melt chocolate and dip half of each cookie. Top with chopped pistachios.

Blueberry Morning Smoothie

INGREDIENTS

- 1 ½ Tbsp macadamia nuts (soaked in water overnight)
- 1/2 cup frozen blueberries
- 1 frozen banana
- 1 Tbsp chia seeds
- 1 Tbsp honey
- 1/4 cup plain greek yogurt
- 3/4 cup whole milk
- Spinach, optional

DIRECTIONS

1. Soak macadamia nuts in water overnight. Drain.
2. Add all ingredients to the blender and blend for 2 minutes or until smooth.

Sweet Tea

INGREDIENTS

- 12 Lipton tea bags
- 4 cups water
- 1/4 tsp baking soda
- 1 ⅓ cup sugar

DIRECTIONS

1. Bring water to a low boil.
2. Remove from heat. Stir in baking soda.
3. Add in tea bags and steep for 15 minutes.
4. Remove tea bags and stir in sugar until dissolved.
5. Transfer to a gallon container and fill with cold water, about 12 more cups.
6. Chill and serve over ice.

Makes one gallon

Note—the baking soda helps cut the bitterness from the black tea.

Chocolate Custard Croissant Bake

INGREDIENTS

- 1/2 cup Nutella
- 1 1/4 cup heavy cream
- 4 egg yolks
- 1/2 cup milk
- 2 Tbsp sugar
- 2 tsp vanilla
- Mini croissants, about 12 oz, can be 1-3 days old
- Raspberries or strawberries to serve

DIRECTIONS

1. Preheat oven to 350 degrees. Grease a 9x13 dish.
2. Add Nutella to a large bowl. Whisk in heavy cream until smooth. Add in egg yolks, milk, sugar, and vanilla. Whisk to fully combine. Add in croissants and toss to coat, let sit 10 minutes, stirring halfway through.
3. Dump in prepared dish and cover with foil. To create a water bath, place pan inside a larger roasting pan and fill the roasting pan with hot water about half way up the side of the 9x13. Be careful not to get any water into the dish. Bake for 50 minutes.
4. Top with raspberries or strawberries. Serve warm.

Note—this can be done without the water bath but the texture may be off, reduce cooking time to 40 minutes if cooking this way.

Try replacing the nutella with 3 mashed ripe bananas and serve with caramel sauce!

Tucker's Eggnog Pie

INGREDIENTS

- Prepared graham cracker pie crust
- 16 oz cream cheese, softened
- 1 cup powdered sugar
- 2 tsp vanilla
- 1/4 cup plain greek yogurt
- 1/4 cup sour cream
- 2/3 cup Egg nog

DIRECTIONS

1. Mix softened cream cheese, powdered sugar, and vanilla with a hand mixer until blended.
2. Add sour cream, yogurt, and eggnog, and blend for 3 minutes or until the mixture is thick and creamy.
3. Pour in prepared graham cracker crust and chill for 4 hours or overnight.
4. Serve cold.

Note—replace eggnog with ¾ cup heavy cream for a traditional no-bake cheesecake.

Buckeyes

INGREDIENTS

- 1 ½ cup creamy peanut butter
- 1/2 cup butter, softened
- 1 tsp vanilla
- 4 cups sifted powdered sugar
- 1/2 cup milk chocolate chips
- 1/2 cup semi sweet chocolate chips
- 1/4 tsp canola oil

DIRECTIONS

1. Combine peanut butter, softened butter, vanilla, and powdered sugar in a bowl. Mix with hands until a dough forms.
2. Shape into small balls, about 2 tsp each. Refrigerate until firm.
3. Add chocolate chips and canola oil to a glass bowl. Microwave 20 seconds. Stir, and microwave in 10 second increments until chocolate is fully melted. Be patient!
4. Use a toothpick to insert peanut butter balls into chocolate until mostly covered.
5. Chill for at least 30 minutes before serving.
6. Go Bucks!

Note—use cylindrical shaped glass for dipping (think shot glass or small children's cup) For an even more professional look, use your finger to smudge the hole that the toothpick made.

Sparkling Vanilla Lemonade

INGREDIENTS

- 2.5 cups water, divided
- 1 cup sugar
- 1 ¼ cup lemon juice, approx. 8 lemons
- 3-4 cups soda water
- 2 tsp vanilla

DIRECTIONS

1. Make the simple syrup. Heat 1 cup water and sugar in a small saucepan until sugar is dissolved. Let cool.
2. Juice lemons and strain out any seeds. Pour into a pitcher.
3. Add simple syrup and 1 ½ cup cold water to the pitcher. Refrigerate until ready to serve.
4. Add vanilla and soda water. Stir and serve over ice.

Note—try with lemon-lime flavored soda water!

Blackberry Lemon Jello Cake

INGREDIENTS

- Box white cake mix
- 3 oz lemon jello
- 1 ½ cup water, divided
- 8 oz cream cheese, room temp
- 1 tsp lemon juice
- 1 tsp vanilla
- 2 Tbsp sugar
- 1/2 pint blackberries
- 8 oz whipped topping

DIRECTIONS

1. Bake cake according to box instructions. Let cool for 15 minutes.
2. Prepare jello mix by adding 1 cup boiling water to the jello until fully dissolved. Add ½ cup cold water.
3. Poke holes all over the cooled cake using a skewer or end of a utensil. Pour liquid jello mixture over the entire cake, making sure it gets into the holes. Refrigerate until set, at least 3 hours.
4. Using a stand or hand mixer, whip the cream cheese, lemon juice, vanilla, and sugar until smooth. Add in blackberries until incorporated. Fold in whipped topping.
5. Top cake with frosting and enjoy!

INGREDIENTS

- 2 ½ cup flour + 9 Tbsp, divided
- 1 tsp salt
- 1 tsp baking baking soda
- 2 sticks unsalted butter
- 1/2 cup white sugar
- 1 cup brown sugar
- 1 egg
- 2 tsp vanilla
- 3 Tbsp raspberry jello mix
- 3 Tbsp orange jello mix
- 1/4 tsp almond extract
- Food coloring, optional
- 1/4 cup sugar

Marble Cookies

DIRECTIONS

1. Combine 2 ½ cups flour, salt, and baking soda. Set aside.
2. Cream butter and both sugars in a stand mixer until fluffy.
3. Add egg and vanilla, mix.
4. Slowly add in dry ingredients on low speed.
5. Once dough is formed, divide into 3 equal parts.
6. Using the bowl used for flour, add 3 Tbsp flour and almond extract to one of the dough balls. Mix with hands, set aside.
7. Add jello mix and 3 Tbsp flour to the remaining two dough balls, use food coloring to get the desired color. Set aside.
8. Preheat the oven to 325 degrees.
9. Using ½ tsp, scoop a small amount of each color and roll into ball marbling as much or as little as you like.
10. Add ¼ cup sugar to a small bowl and coat each cookie.
11. Place on baking sheet at least 1 inch apart.
12. Bake for about 12 minutes. Transfer to a cooling rack.

Note—use any color or jello flavor you want - try Neapolitan; red, white, and blue; or red, white, and green for Christmas!

Smores Cookies

INGREDIENTS

- 10 full graham crackers
- Pack of six Hershey's chocolate bars
- 20 large marshmallows
- 36 oz Tollhouse cookie dough

DIRECTIONS

1. Preheat oven to 350 degrees.
2. Line a large baking sheet with parchment paper, you do not want to skip this step!
3. Break graham cracker in half and place 6 on baking sheet, top each with 3 Hershey's squares. Rip marshmallow in half and place the sticky side down. Take about 1 ½ Tbsp of cookie dough and form into an egg shape. Place over top and around the sides of the marshmallows to avoid toppling over while baking.
4. Bake for 14-16 minutes, checking after a few minutes to adjust any that may have fallen over. Remove from the oven and quickly reshape the cookies into circles with a spatula. Let cool on baking sheet for 5 minutes before transferring to cooling rack.

88   *Makes 20 large cookies*

INGREDIENTS

- 1-2 small honey crisp apples
- 1/2 tsp cinnamon
- 1/4 cup white sugar
- 1/4 cup brown sugar
- 1/4 cup flour for rolling
- Refrigerated crescent dough sheets
- 4 Tbsp butter, softened
- 3/4 cup freshly shredded cheddar cheese

Note—if you cannot find crescent dough sheets, crescent dough rolls will work just fine. Simply pinch seems before rolling out.

Apple Cheddar Cruffins

DIRECTIONS

1. Preheat oven to 350 degrees.
2. Slice apples into very thin slices. Mix cinnamon and both sugars together, set aside.
3. Sprinkle flour on a flat surface. Roll out one sheet of dough at a time.
4. Brush the entire pastry sheet with softened butter, sprinkle with 2 Tbsp cinnamon sugar mixture, top with thinly sliced apples and cheese. Use photos for reference.
5. Starting at the bottom, roll the dough longways creating a log. Cut in half. Cut each half longways exposing the layers, creating 4 pieces per sheet. Roll each one with the layers facing up. Place in muffin tin and repeat with remaining dough sheets.
6. Sprinkle cruffins with any leftover cinnamon sugar mixture and bake for 25 minutes.

Makes 12 cruffins

Energy Colada

INGREDIENTS

- 8.4 oz can Rockstar Energy Drink
- 2 Tbsp Torani pineapple syrup
- 2 Tbsp Torani coconut syrup
- 4 Tbsp heavy cream
- Ice

DIRECTIONS

1. Pour the Rockstar in a large glass.
2. Stir in syrups.
3. Slowly stir in heavy cream, add ice.
4. Enjoy!

Note—using sugar-free or a different brand energy drink may cause the cream to curdle. Follow the recipe on this one!

Acknowledgements

To the One who makes all things possible - thank you for who You are and who You have called me to be. You have been so, so good to me.

Joel - if we get down to it, this all started with you. Your encouragement has given me the freedom to be adventurous in the kitchen, which has led to my confidence in experimentation and risks that I may have never taken. Good thing you like pizza! Thank you for supporting me through this book, and lastly, thank you for doing the dishes. I love you so.

Tucker & Tenley - thank you for being my forever taste testers. You make this journey so much sweeter.

Redstone Arsenal employees/Joel's coworkers - thank you for trusting me to cook lunches for you for two whole years. It was an honor to share my ideas with you and your feedback meant the world to me.

To my church family, friends, and neighbors - thank you for willingly tasting all my creations, for your honest review, and most importantly, not letting anything go to waste. I appreciate all the support!

Made in the USA
Columbia, SC
08 January 2025

51398883R00054